When Santa Made Me Cry

15 Heartbreaking Stories that Happened on Christmas Eve

By Hollie Dayes

TABLE OF CONTENTS

DISCLAIMER

The stories contained within this collection are inspired by real-life experiences and events that have profoundly impacted the author. However, to uphold the privacy and confidentiality of those involved, names and specific identifying details have been changed or omitted. This measure has been taken to ensure that the dignity and personal lives of individuals are respected.

These narratives intend to reflect genuine emotions and experiences while honoring the complex realities faced by those depicted. While every effort has been made to maintain the accuracy and integrity of the events described, the author recognizes the importance of safeguarding the identities of those who have played a role in their journey.

As such, readers are invited to engage with these stories as explorations of human emotion, resilience, and connection, without compromising the privacy of the individuals who inspired them. Thank you for understanding the necessity of these changes to preserve the integrity of the narrative and the individuals within it.

TRIGGER WARNING

This book contains content that may be distressing for some readers. Within its pages, you will encounter scenes involving guns, and blood, and it delves into profound themes of loss and grief.

We urge readers to approach these stories with caution and to prioritize their emotional well-being. If you find yourself affected by these themes, or if you or someone you know is struggling with related issues, we encourage you to seek professional support or counseling. Remember, you are not alone, and there are resources available to help you navigate these difficult emotions.

To all who have endured the weight of life's unfair timing, whose plans and dreams were shattered by circumstances beyond their control— this is for you.

This book is dedicated to all those who, like the individuals in these stories, have found themselves caught in the wrong timing of events and circumstances.

May God bless you with the strength to rise above the struggles, and with faith that carries you through the darkest moments. Your courage in the face of adversity is a testament to the human spirit, and I hope that brighter days lie ahead, even when the path seems steep.

INTRODUCTION

When Santa Made Me Cry is a collection of 15 heartfelt stories that take a deeper look at Christmas Eve, a night often wrapped in joy and warmth, but for many, tinged with sorrow and loss. These stories peel back the layers of holiday cheer to reveal the bittersweet emotions that can lie beneath—the moments when the magic of the season collides with the harsh realities of life.

In these pages, you will find tales of people whose lives are forever changed on what should be the happiest night of the year. From heartache and unexpected tragedy to the quiet courage that rises in the face of adversity, each story brings to light the fragile hope that often flickers in times of darkness. Christmas, a season meant for celebration, becomes a backdrop for the exploration of loss, betrayal, and resilience.

Though tears fall in the midst of twinkling lights and festive gatherings, *When Santa Made Me Cry* is also a testament to the strength of the human spirit. It reminds us that even in our most vulnerable moments, we can find solace, healing, and perhaps a renewed sense of purpose. These stories capture not only the heartbreak that can shadow the season but also the quiet grace that comes with accepting life's challenges, offering a glimpse of hope even in the most difficult times.

"All though the world is full of suffering,
It is also full of overcoming."

-Helen Keller

Story 1:

The Silent Cradle

It was supposed to be the Christmas they had dreamed of for ten long years. Emily and David had waited, prayed, and endured heartache after heartache, but on December 20, their miracle finally arrived—a beautiful baby boy. The hospital room was filled with joy, love, and tears of happiness. They were finally parents. As Christmas Eve approached, they were released to take their precious child home, their hearts full, ready to celebrate the holidays as a family.

Family and friends filled their homes, eager to welcome the new baby. The house was warm with laughter and Christmas cheer, the tree lit with twinkling lights, gifts stacked high beneath it. Everything felt perfect. Emily couldn't stop smiling as she cradled her son, her heart overflowing with love and gratitude. This was the moment they had prayed for, a dream come true.

As the night wore on, Emily took her baby upstairs to change him into a little Christmas onesie she had saved for this very night. She hummed softly as she undressed him, her heart full, when suddenly... something felt wrong. His skin was cold. His tiny chest wasn't rising. Panic gripped her, her breath catching in her throat as she shook him gently, calling his name. But there was no sound, no movement.

Her screams pierced the air. David rushed into the room, his face full of fear, but it was too late. Their baby was gone—taken silently in his sleep by SIDS (Sudden Infant Death Syndrome). The room that had been filled with hope and joy moments ago now felt unbearably empty.

The sounds of Christmas—laughter, carols, the crackling fire—vanished, replaced by sobs, by disbelief, by the agonizing realization that their miracle had been stolen away. Emily collapsed to the floor, clutching the tiny lifeless body of the child they had waited for all these years, while David fell to his knees beside her, his heart breaking.

What should have been the happiest night of their lives became a night of unbearable sorrow. The joy of Christmas shattered into pieces, as their long-awaited miracle was ripped from them, leaving only silence, grief, and the cold, cruel reality of loss. The lights on the tree twinkled on, oblivious to the devastation that had darkened their world.

"Joy and loss can arrive in the same breath, reminding us how fragile life truly is, even in moments meant for celebration."

-Hollie Dayes

<u>In a nutshell</u>: This story highlights the heartbreaking contrast between the joy and celebration of the newborn's arrival and the overwhelming sense of loss that follows. The title reflects both how fragile life can be and the deep sorrow that comes when tragedy strikes without warning.

"You will lose someone you can't live without, and your heart will be badly broken, and the bad news is that you never completely get over the loss of your beloved. But this is also the good news. They live forever in your broken heart that doesn't seal back up. And you come through. It's like having a broken leg that never heals perfectly — that still hurts when the weather gets cold, but you learn to dance with the limp."

-Anne Lamott

Story 2:

Moments Too Late

On a bitterly cold winter night, a daughter boards a flight, her heart alight with anticipation. She's determined to surprise her single mother for Christmas Eve, longing to revive the joy of their shared holiday traditions. She imagines the glow of lights, the scent of freshly baked cookies, and the laughter that would fill their home once again.

Just moments away from her mother's doorstep, her phone rings and time seems to stand still. The voice on the other end delivers a devastating blow—her mother has died in a tragic car accident, racing to buy a last-minute gift for her beloved daughter, the child she had longed for and prayed would come home this year.

Standing on her mother's doorstep, gifts clutched tightly in her hands, she feels an overwhelming wave of despair wash over her. The bright lights of the holiday decorations mock her with their cheer, while she stands frozen in the frigid air, her dreams turned to ash.

Each second stretches into eternity as she fights to comprehend the enormity of her loss. The door is closed, not just to the house, but to a lifetime of memories yet to be made. The holiday she envisioned, filled with love and laughter, transforms into a haunting reminder of what could have been. In that devastating moment, the warmth of Christmas is swallowed by a chilling emptiness, marking a night of joy that has turned into the darkest sorrow.

"One moment of hope can vanish in a heartbeat, leaving behind a lifetime of sorrow and the ache of what could have been."

-Hollie Dayes

<u>In a nutshell</u>: This story highlights the deep sadness of a missed opportunity and how tragic timing can change a person's life forever. What was meant to be a joyful surprise for the daughter quickly turns into an unbearable loss. The title conveys the emotional impact of the story and the harsh twist of fate that leads to such heartache.

"Every soldier must know, before he goes into battle, how the little battle he is to fight fits into the larger picture, and how the success of his fighting will influence the battle as a whole."

-Bernard Law Montgomery

Story 3:

Shattered Homecoming

After six grueling months on the battlefield, an army soldier finally returns home, worn down but filled with excitement. He imagines the look of joy on her face when he surprises her with thoughtful gifts and stories of his time away. His heart is filled with hope as he approaches their front door, envisioning a night of laughter, love, and the rekindling of their shared dreams.

But the moment he enters, everything he holds dear crumbles before him. The air feels heavy with betrayal as he discovers that his wife has been unfaithful. In a cruel twist of fate, she's pregnant with another man's child. The realization hits him like a punch to the gut—his heart sinks as he realizes that everything he fought for—every lonely night, every moment of longing—has been in vain.

Instead of a joyous Christmas filled with laughter and love, he is left standing in a shattered home, surrounded by the remnants of a life that no longer exists. The gifts he brought for her feel like stones in his hands, symbols of a future that has been cruelly snatched away. His heart aches with an unbearable grief, mourning not just the loss of his wife, but the dreams they had built together, now lost in the bitter cold of betrayal.

"Sometimes, the joy of coming home hides the pain of betrayal."

-Hollie Dayes

<u>In a nutshell</u>: In this story about the emotional devastation of the soldier's return, is met with crushing disappointment as the love and reunion he hoped for are overshadowed by betrayal and heartbreak. The title captures the deep sense of loss he feels, not only for his relationship but also for the life he thought he was coming back to.

"A hero is someone who has given his or her life to something bigger than oneself."

– Joseph Campbell

Story 4:

The Weight of Absence

On Christmas Eve, a retired army woman sits in silence, her heart heavy as she stares at the empty chair where her beloved son once sat. This is the first holiday without him, and the void he left feels unbearable. Their bond was a fortress, unbreakable and filled with love, but now it lies in ruins after the tragic loss that shattered her world.

As the night wears on, the weight of his absence feels heavier, pressing down on her heart. Memories flood her mind—laughs shared, dreams spoken, love exchanged. But now, it's just her, alone in a house that feels cold and empty without him. The loneliness wraps around her like a suffocating blanket, and she can't find a way to push through the overwhelming sorrow.

The house, once alive with the spirit of Christmas, feels like a cold prison, echoing her despair. She tries to cling to the spirit of the holiday, but it feels like a cruel joke—decorations that once brought joy now mock her pain. With each passing hour, the emptiness becomes suffocating, and she is haunted by the thought that she has buried her child before her own time.

In a moment of utter desperation, overwhelmed by grief and despair, she takes a step that she can't take back. With trembling hands and a shattered heart, she picks up a gun, hoping to silence the torment that has consumed her. As she pulls the trigger, the echo of the shot pierces the silence of the night, a tragic farewell to a world that has become too painful to endure.

Christmas morning dawns bright and beautiful, but inside her home lies the stark reality of loss. Her lifeless body is found, a heartbreaking reminder of a love that once flourished but has now crumbled under the weight of sorrow. The holiday, meant for joy and family, becomes a haunting testament to the depths of grief—a mother's tragic end in a world stripped of her son, leaving behind a legacy of love and a void that can never be filled.

"In the silence of loss, even the brightest Christmas can feel like the darkest night."

-Hollie Dayes

In a nutshell: This story captures the deep sadness and emotional struggle a retired army woman faces after losing her son. The title highlights how significantly his death affects her life, especially during a season meant for joy and family togetherness. It emphasizes the depth of her sorrow and the heartbreaking results of her loneliness and isolation.

"Throughout my life, there were a few hard days. Days where even when I tried to be happy, my heart still cracked, and Mother's Day was one of those. For others, it stood as a celebration. For me, it spoke of loss and failure."

— Brittainy C. Cherry

Story 5:

Echoes of a Lost Christmas

On a frigid Christmas Eve, a devoted mother enters the chaotic swirl of a packed shopping mall, her heart alive with love and anticipation as she prepares to make her daughter's holiday magical. Three years old and full of energy, her little girl dances at her side, excitement radiating from her bright smile. The air is thick with laughter and the scent of cinnamon, promising a night of warmth and joy.

But in a harrowing instant, everything changes. As the mother glances away to check her shopping list, she turns back to find her daughter gone, swallowed by the throng of bustling holiday shoppers. Panic grips her heart like a vice, a cold wave of terror crashing over her. "Where are you?" she cries, her voice lost in the cacophony of festive sounds. Each passing moment feels like an eternity as she searches every corner, calling out her daughter's name, her heart racing with fear.

Then, in a moment that will haunt her forever, she sees it: a stranger leading her daughter away, the little girl's tiny hand grasped firmly in his. A scream catches in her throat, and time freezes. She charges forward, but the crowd closes in around her like a dark wave, pulling her away from the most important thing in her life. The joy of the holiday season crumbles into a nightmare.

Days stretch into weeks, and the search ends in despair; her daughter is gone, taken from her in the blink of an eye. The joyous celebrations of Christmas morph into a chilling reminder of her loss, each carol and twinkling light a dagger in her heart. Five years later, the mother still wakes up in a cold sweat, replaying that fateful moment over and over in her mind, trapped in a cycle of guilt and heartbreak.

Every Christmas, she walks through the same mall, the laughter of families around her a bitter echo of her own. She feels invisible, a ghost haunted by memories of the little girl who once filled her world with light. Each holiday season only deepens her sorrow, as she navigates a reality where the joy she once knew is forever lost, leaving her alone in a world that celebrates love while she mourns the child she can never hold again.

"Amid holiday cheer, a single moment of distraction can turn joy into an endless ache, reminding us that love can be as fragile as the twinkling lights that decorate our lives."

-Hollie Dayes

In a nutshell: This title encapsulates the enduring pain and haunting memories of the mother's loss, highlighting how the joy of the holiday is overshadowed by the trauma of that fateful day.
It reflects the lasting impact of her daughter's disappearance, resonating through the years as she grapples with grief and the longing for what once was.

"By the time a man realizes that maybe his father was right, he usually has a son who thinks he's wrong."

-Charles Wadsworth

Story 6:

Christmas in Shadows

On a cold Christmas Eve, a once-bright young man finds himself consumed by the relentless grip of addiction, a shadow of the person he used to be. As the festive lights twinkle around him, he feels more alone than ever, trapped in a cycle of despair that pushes him further from the loving family who once held him close. Desperation gnaws at him, driving him to the unthinkable: he breaks into his parents' home, searching for anything of value to feed his insatiable need for drugs.

Heart pounding, he rummages through familiar rooms filled with memories—old photographs, toys from his childhood, and the comforting scent of home. He fills his pockets with stolen treasures: a gold watch, some cash, and his mother's beloved jewelry. Just as he thinks he can escape the dark reality of his life, the front door creaks open, and in walks his father, a beacon of hope, carrying bags of groceries and holiday cheer.

Seeing his son in the driveway sends a jolt through him. "Please, son, let's talk," he pleads, eyes filled with love and worry. "I've missed you. Come home. We can make this right." But the son, trapped in a haze of panic and shame, feels the walls closing in around him. The warm glow of the Christmas lights now feels like a spotlight exposing his darkest truths.

In a moment of blind rage and fear, he lashes out, striking his father. The sound of the blow echoes through the night, followed by an unbearable silence as his father crumples to the ground —lifeless.

A wave of horror crashes over him, and the realization of what he has done floods his mind. He doesn't know whether to scream or cry, but all he can do is run. He flees into the night, leaving behind a life shattered by violence and addiction, his heart pounding with guilt and grief.

Four years pass, but the memories of that fateful Christmas Eve haunt him, an inescapable nightmare replaying in his mind. Each holiday season is a painful reminder of the father he betrayed and the family he destroyed. The joy of Christmas, once filled with love and laughter, is now a chilling reminder of his past, a constant ache in his chest that won't go away. He longs for redemption, grappling with the weight of his actions, thinking that the bond severed by his moment of rage can never be repaired. The festive spirit is forever overshadowed by the darkness of that night, leaving him to face a world stripped of the love he once had.

"On a night meant for love and joy,
I chose desperation over family. In a
single moment, I lost everything I held
dear, leaving behind a father's love that
I can never reclaim."

-Hollie Dayes

<u>In a nutshell</u>: This story sparks the
contrasts between the holiday's
intended joy and the tragic events
that unfold, highlighting how the
darkness of addiction and betrayal
can overshadow moments that should
be filled with love and celebration.
It reflects the deep emotional
turmoil and haunting memories of a
regretful son that linger long after the
holiday has passed.

"It's ok to be grumpy sometimes, to have bad days to struggle, to make mistakes, to say the wrong thing, feel overwhelmed and under-appreciated, to be out-of-sorts and sort-of-over-it all. It's ok for us big humans, and it's ok for our little humans, too. After all, we're all humans, right? How else will our little humans learn that it's okay to be human? Remember, we're imperfect humans growing imperfect humans in an imperfect world, and that's perfectly okay."

— L. R. Knost

Story 7:

Fading Christmas

In the whirlwind of the holiday season, a devoted mother of two young toddlers is swept up in a chaotic storm of school plays, concerts, and endless preparations. With each passing day, she pours herself into making everything perfect for her children, convinced that the fatigue is just the price of motherhood. As Christmas Eve approaches, her body finally succumbs to the relentless exhaustion, but she brushes off her weariness, telling herself it's merely the toll of sleepless nights and the chaos that defines her life.

Yet this time, something feels different. With a heavy heart, she decides to visit the doctor, seeking reassurance that a little rest will be all she needs to regain her strength. But instead of comfort, she receives a crushing blow: stage 4 breast cancer. The diagnosis lands like a thunderstorm in her mind, drowning out the joy that should fill the air with holiday cheer. What should have been a night brimming with laughter, love, and twinkling lights turns into a moment of heart-wrenching clarity.

Returning home, she feels like a ghost, walking through the house that is supposed to be filled with warmth. The air is thick with a suffocating silence, amplifying the joyous laughter of her toddlers, which now feels like an echo from a world she might soon leave behind. Christmas, once her favorite time of year, becomes a brutal reminder of the life she might not be able to witness as her children grow.

As she sits in the dim glow of the Christmas tree lights, the weight of her diagnosis settles heavily on her heart, each flicker reminding her of moments she may never share. The thought of leaving her little ones without their mother tears at her soul, and the magic of the season dissolves into a landscape of despair. This Christmas, instead of feeling the warmth of family and love, she is engulfed in the icy grip of fear and sorrow.

What was meant to be a night of joy becomes her most devastating hour, as she grapples with the reality of her future—a future that now hangs by a thread, dimmed by the shadows of a disease that threatens to steal everything she holds dear. She longs for the chance to cradle her children one last time, to read them bedtime stories, and to watch them unwrap gifts with sparkling eyes. The ticking clock in the background becomes a relentless reminder of time slipping away, leaving her to navigate a holiday marked by heartbreak and the unbearable weight of uncertainty.

"Amidst the twinkling lights and festive cheer, a mother's heart shatters as she faces the grim reality of her diagnosis, transforming every moment with her children into a precious, yet painful memory of love that may soon fade away."

-Hollie Dayes

In a nutshell: This story captures the heartbreaking contrast between the holiday's joyful expectations and the mother's devastating diagnosis, reflecting the slow realization that her time with her children may be slipping away. It evokes the sense of fading hope and the emotional weight of a Christmas overshadowed by the fragility of life.

"Anyone that's been in the place of wanting another child or wanting a child knows the disappointment, the pain, and the loss that you go through trying and struggling with infertility."

– Nicole Kidman

Story 8:

The Last Hope

Emma had dreamed of this moment for years. After countless doctor visits, hormone treatments, and four failed IVF attempts, this was her last chance—the fifth and final embryo. Just days ago, she had cried tears of joy when the pregnancy test came back positive. Finally, after all the heartache and waiting, it seemed her miracle had arrived. Her heart swelled with excitement as she imagined telling her family, picturing the looks of joy on their faces when they heard the news.

As Christmas Eve approached, she was ready for her big announcement, her heart soaring with hope. Before gathering with loved ones, she decided to take one last test to reassure herself that everything was on track. But when she looked down at the result, her world stopped—the test was negative. Panic surged through her as she frantically called her doctor, desperately clinging to the hope that it was a mistake. But then came the words she had feared most: she had lost the baby to a chemical pregnancy. The tiny life she had already begun to love had slipped away before it could truly begin.

The shock of the loss crushed her. The child she had fought so hard to conceive, the dream she had poured all her hopes into, was gone. What was meant to be the happiest Christmas of her life had become her worst nightmare. She sat alone in the quiet house, surrounded by unopened gifts, each one a painful reminder of the future that had been so ruthlessly taken from her.

Outside, the world continued to celebrate. Christmas lights twinkled in the windows of neighbors' homes, and laughter echoed through the night. But inside, her world had shattered. The joyful anticipation she had felt just days before now seemed like a distant memory, replaced by an aching emptiness that hollowed her out. She had imagined this Christmas would be the start of a new chapter, filled with hope and promise. Instead, it had become a night of unimaginable grief, the weight of her final loss pressing down on her like an unbearable burden.

As the hours passed, the festive sounds of the holiday felt like cruel reminders of the joy she would never experience. The dream of holding her child, of watching them grow, had been ripped from her grasp, leaving her to face a future filled with the painful absence of a life she would never know. And on that Christmas Eve, in the shadow of what could have been, all that remained was the deep, unrelenting ache of a mother's broken heart.

"She dreamed of a miracle, only to be left with the quiet emptiness of dreams that faded too soon."

-Hollie Dayes

<u>In a nutshell</u>: This title reflects the profound loss and sorrow the woman feels after her last hope of becoming a mother is shattered. It captures the emotional emptiness she experiences; contrasting the joy she had envisioned with the heartbreaking reality of her loss, all set against the backdrop of Christmas.

"All you can do is hope, at the end of the road, that you've given your kids enough life lessons [so when] it's time for them to live their life, they can flourish on their own because they're going to have to make their own path as well. Even though we've set them up in the best way possible. And the same thing applies to being a husband. When you know you're committed, everything else takes care of itself."

-LeBron James

Story 9:

A House of Broken Dreams

A small family, eager for a fresh start, moves into their new home just weeks before Christmas. The house, though modest, feels like a dream come true. It's their chance to build something lasting, a place to make new memories and leave the struggles of the past behind. They decorate it with care, stringing up lights and setting out presents, the warmth of the season filling every corner. The children laugh, their mother hums holiday tunes, and for the first time in a long while, the father feels at peace.

On Christmas Eve, as the family basks in the glow of the tree, the father steps aside to open a letter he's been anxiously awaiting. His hands shake with anticipation. This letter, he believes, will confirm everything—the financial breakthrough that will carry them through the holidays and into a brighter future.

But the moment he reads the words, his heart sinks. It's not a blessing, but a curse. The letter reveals a $50,000 lien on their home, an overlooked detail that now threatens to take everything from them. If they can't pay, they'll lose the house—everything they've worked for, every bit of security they thought they had, will be gone.

He stands in the doorway, frozen, his hands trembling, while behind him, his wife and children remain wrapped up in the holiday's illusion of joy. They're still laughing, unaware of the disaster that's about to crash down around them. The tree's lights blink cheerfully, but to him, they feel cruel and hollow, mocking the devastation that now grips his heart.

His throat tightens, and tears well in his eyes as he watches his family, knowing he can't bear to ruin this moment for them—this fleeting bit of happiness before the storm swallows them whole. The home they had just begun to fill with love is slipping through his fingers, and the joy of Christmas turns into a haunting reminder of how fragile their dreams truly are. The night, once so full of hope and warmth, is now shadowed by a grief he doesn't know how to face, leaving him standing in the doorway, consumed by a loss too heavy to bear.

"Sometimes the home we build in our hearts crumbles long before the walls fall down."

-Hollie Dayes

<u>In a nutshell</u>: The story reflects the crushing devastation the family faces on the night before Christmas when the unexpected news shatters their dreams of a new beginning. It captures the emotional weight of a moment that should be filled with joy but instead, it is marked by heartbreak and uncertainty.

"Only people who are capable of loving strongly can also suffer great sorrow, but this same necessity of loving serves to counteract their grief and heals them."

– Leo Tolstoy

Story 10:

A Mother's Final Prayer

On Christmas Eve, the sterile hospital room felt like a tomb to a single mother consumed by unbearable grief. Just one year had passed since she buried her two older sons, both stolen away by the same merciless disease that now gripped her youngest, John. At 24, he lay fragile and weak, fighting a losing battle against stage 4 lung cancer, his spirit flickering like the dying light on the Christmas tree just beyond the window.

As laughter and merriment echoed faintly from the holiday celebrations outside, she knelt beside John's bed, heart heavy with despair. She whispered prayers into the silence, her hopes floating away like snowflakes in the bitter wind. Each labored breath he took felt like a countdown to an inevitable goodbye, and the memories of their shared laughter haunted her. The warmth of family dinners and holiday traditions now seemed like distant dreams, swallowed by the shadow of loss.

The acrid smell of antiseptic mingled with the rhythmic beeping of machines, a cruel reminder of the fragility of life. Despite the pain etched across his face, John mustered a weak smile, eyes glistening with a flicker of hope that made her heartache. "Mom, don't leave me," he whispered, his voice fragile, as if it might shatter under the weight of their reality.

For a brief hour, they laughed and shared stories, stealing moments of joy from the abyss of sorrow that threatened to engulf them. Each smile felt like a precious gift, a fleeting escape from the cruel fate that loomed over them. But as the clock ticked closer to midnight, she could see his strength slipping away, his laughter dimming as fatigue settled in. The warmth that had filled the room turned cold, leaving only the chilling silence that wrapped around her heart like a vice.

With tears cascading down her cheeks, she held his frail hand, desperate to anchor him to this world. "Please, John, don't go," she pleaded, her voice breaking with anguish. As midnight approached, his gaze turned distant, and in a voice barely above a whisper, he murmured, "I'm tired, Mom. I can't fight anymore." In that harrowing moment, he slipped away, leaving her with the unbearable silence that filled the room and echoed in her heart.

When the clock struck twelve, it not only marked the arrival of Christmas but shattered her last connection to joy. Instead of laughter and love, the room was suffocated by sorrow, the once warm and inviting space now a haunting reminder of what she had lost.

She collapsed into a heap of broken dreams and shattered hopes, the weight of her grief pressing down on her chest like a thousand-pound stone. Christmas, once a time for celebration, now felt like a bitter curse—a painful reminder of the family she fought so hard to keep together, now reduced to memories that cut deeper than any blade.

In the flickering lights of the Christmas tree, she realized that her holiday spirit had been extinguished, forever darkened by the loss of her three precious sons. The season of joy had turned into a season of mourning, and as she sat alone in the sterile room, she knew that the echoes of their laughter would never again fill her heart, leaving her to navigate a world forever altered by grief and sorrow, lost to the cruel hands of fate.

"In the stillness of Christmas Eve, she held onto memories of her lost sons, their laughter mingling with the sterile sounds of the hospital. Each moment was a reminder of the laughter that once filled their home, now replaced by silence and sorrow. Illuminating a world that had moved on while her heart remained shattered, mourning not just one son, but the precious memories of three."

-Hollie Dayes

<u>In a nutshell</u>: This story captures the profound darkness that envelops the mother as she faces the unbearable loss of her youngest son on a day meant for celebration and joy. It emphasizes the absence of hope and

warmth that typically accompanies the holiday, reflecting the deep sorrow and emptiness she experiences in the wake of her heartbreak.

"Your enemies are not so far from you. They laugh with you; they give you advice and they eat with you. God exposes them."

— Gugu Mofokeng

Story 11:

A Gift of Betrayal

Teresa had spent years chasing her dream, pouring her heart and soul into her work until every sacrifice felt worth it. When she finally secured a job abroad, it was like the sun breaking through a storm. With her visa approved and her bags packed, she counted down the days until she would board her flight. But then, life threw a wrench in her plans. Unexpected delays forced her to reschedule, and the only seats left were on a flight set for Christmas Eve—a bittersweet compromise that felt more like a punishment than a celebration.

As she touched down amidst the festive chaos of the holiday season, her heart swelled with anticipation, picturing the life she would build in her new country. But that joy shattered when customs officers at the airport discovered a hidden stash of cocaine in her luggage. The ground seemed to fall away beneath her feet as panic gripped her heart. Confusion morphed into disbelief as she was taken to an airport jail, the vibrant holiday spirit outside her cell fading into a blur of despair.

Sitting on the cold, hard bench, Teresa's mind raced. How had this happened? The life she had fought so hard to achieve was slipping through her fingers like sand. Her thoughts spiraled into a darker abyss when she discovered

the truth: her cousin, consumed by
envy over her success, had planted the
drugs in her bag, hoping to sabotage
her future. The betrayal cut deeper than
any wound; not only had she lost her
freedom, but she had also lost the bond
of trust with a family member she had
once loved fiercely.

In that stark, sterile cell, Teresa felt
as if the walls were closing in on her.
Memories of laughter and warmth
from family gatherings, once so
vivid, were now haunted by this cruel
twist of fate. She imagined how her
Christmas should have been, filled with
joy, new beginnings, and the promise
of a brighter future. Instead, she was
surrounded by cold metal bars, a
chilling reminder of her cousin's malice
and her shattered dreams. The clock
ticked relentlessly, marking time she
could not reclaim.

What should have been a Christmas of hope and renewal became a haunting reminder of betrayal and despair, leaving Teresa to grapple with the crushing weight of brokenness and loss. Her future, once vibrant and full of potential, now felt as distant as the holiday cheer that echoed outside her cell. In that moment of profound sorrow, Teresa realized she was not just fighting for her freedom; she was fighting to hold onto the pieces of herself that her cousin had so ruthlessly tried to destroy.

"In a world filled with dreams, betrayal can turn joy into a prison."

-Hollie Dayes

In a nutshell: This title evokes the contrast between the festive season and Teresa, the protagonist's devastating experience, where what should have been a season of hope and joy is marred by treachery. It highlights the irony of her hopes for a bright future being overshadowed by betrayal and despair, suggesting that even in a season of joy, darkness can lurk beneath the surface.

"Saving one dog will not change the world, but surely for that one dog, the world will change forever."

– Karen Davison

Story 12:

A Christmas Without Mercy

In a harsh Arab country where Christmas is merely a distant whisper, Eva walks the streets with a heavy heart, surrounded by the suffering of stray dogs that roam desperately for scraps of kindness. In a society where cruelty toward these innocent creatures is commonplace, she bears witness to the horrifying reality: police routinely hunt down stray dogs, leaving them to suffer alone in agony. The heartless indifference of her community only deepens her resolve to protect those who cannot defend themselves.

In a society that shows no regard for animal rights, despite her limited means, she dedicates her meager income and free time to feeding the abandoned dogs she has grown to love. Eva feels a deep calling to make a difference, no matter how small. Each meal she provides is a small act of kindness amidst a world that views these creatures as pests to be eradicated.

As Christmas Eve approaches, Eva decides to prepare a special feast for her furry friends. With careful planning, she cooks a heartfelt meal, yearning to give them a moment of joy in a world filled with suffering. After months of sneaking food to her beloved strays, she finds a secluded spot behind a house to safely feed them, hoping for a peaceful gathering.

But as she arrives, the scene turns into a nightmare. As the dogs excitedly rush toward her, tails wagging in excitement and love. The police arrive, brandishing guns. In an act of unthinkable cruelty, they draw their weapons, their faces cold and unyielding. In a heart-wrenching moment, they open fire, taking the lives of the innocent animals right in front of her. Eva's screams pierce the air, filled with anguish and disbelief, as the brutality of the situation overwhelms her. Eva screams in horror, her heart breaking as she witnesses the massacre unfold before her eyes. She watches in horror as the bodies of the innocent dogs she has fought so hard to protect fall one by one. The police leave without a word, leaving her surrounded by the lifeless bodies of the strays she cared for so deeply.

Devastated, she lies among them, heartbroken and consumed by the profound injustice she has just witnessed. Tears stream down her face as she cradles their bodies, her anguish palpable in the stillness of the night. In that moment, she grapples with the profound evil of humanity, questioning how a society can turn a blind eye to such cruelty. How can a world turn so cold, so callous? This Christmas Eve, instead of celebrating joy and love, she is left to mourn the lives lost and the innocence shattered, forever changed by the brutal reality of the world around her.

"In a land where kindness is a crime, one woman's love shines bright, even as darkness closes in."

-Hollie Dayes

<u>In a nutshell</u>: This title captures the essence of Eva's heartbreaking experience, emphasizing the clash between her kindness toward the stray dogs and the brutal reality of the world around her. It reflects the theme of innocence destroyed by indifference and violence, highlighting the profound emotional impact of her story during what should be a season of joy and love.

"If you truly want to be respected by people you love, you must prove to them that you can survive without them."

– Michael Bassey Johnson

Story 13:

The Abandoned Vows

On December 24, 2018, Erika stood before an altar adorned with flowers and candles, her heart fluttering with joy and anticipation. Today was to be the celebration of their love, a beautiful milestone marking four incredible years together. With their wedding just a year away, she had imagined this day filled with laughter, love, and dreams of a future intertwined.

But as the minutes turned into hours, the man she loved was nowhere to be found. Panic coursed through her veins, her heart racing as she scanned the crowd, each face a reminder of his absence. Friends and family gathered, their smiles slowly fading into worried glances. The cheerful music that once filled the air began to sound distant, replaced by an echoing silence that deepened her dread.

Time stretched painfully as the groom's parents joined her frantic search, their concern mirrored in her own. Just as her hope began to wither, she caught sight of a letter lying atop their wedding cake, the cruel words like a dagger to her heart. With trembling hands, she opened it, her breath hitching as she read the shaky handwriting.

He was sorry. He had abandoned her. The weight of his fear and doubts poured from the page, the finality of his decision crashing over her like an unforgiving wave. He had fled the country, leaving her alone at the altar, the promises of forever crumbling into dust around her.

Erika felt the ground shift beneath her feet as despair engulfed her. All the dreams they had nurtured together—planning their future, envisioning a family—were now ashes, leaving her standing in a cruel reality. The vibrant decorations, once symbols of their love, transformed into mocking reminders of a celebration that would never be. Tears streamed down her face as the truth settled in, her heart shattering with each drop that fell.

The joyous atmosphere around her faded into a blur, replaced by the haunting silence of abandonment. What should have been a day of joy was now a nightmare, a painful reminder of the man who had vowed to love her but instead chose to leave her broken. The laughter of the guests felt like distant echoes, mocking her in the very space that was supposed to be filled with happiness.

In that moment, Erika was left to confront the crushing reality of her loss, surrounded by the remnants of a life that could have been. She stood alone, forever marked by the betrayal of the man who was supposed to be her forever, mourning not just the love lost, but the future that had been ripped away in an instant.

"On what should have been the happiest day of her life, she stood alone, her heart breaking under the weight of a love that vanished in front of the altar."

-Hollie Dayes

<u>In a nutshell</u>: This story encapsulates the tragedy of Erika, the bride's tragic experience, emphasizing the anticipation of a joyful celebration that turns into a heartbreaking disappointment. It evokes a sense of longing and loss, reflecting the shattered dreams of love and commitment that were never realized.

"Mom used to say we were the same soul split in two and walking around on four legs. It seems unnatural being born together and then dying apart."

— Melodie Ramone

Story 14:

Tears of a Twin

On Christmas Eve, Nora, a devoted flight attendant whose heart swells with excitement and anticipation for the arrival of her twin sister's first child. After years of yearning, they had planned this moment together, each dreaming of the joy and laughter that a new life would bring. Nora has arranged her holiday schedule to be by her sister's side, ready to embrace the joy of motherhood and sisterhood all over again.

As she boards a full flight, Nora's gaze falls upon two twin girls cuddled together, clutching their favorite teddy bears, a bittersweet reminder of her cherished childhood memories with her sister. The innocence of the moment tugs at her heart, stirring up a longing that dances between nostalgia and joy.

As the flight progresses, a sudden scream shatters the stillness. Rushing to the source, Nora finds one of the girls in tears, desperate for her lost teddy bear that has slipped beneath the seat. As she retrieves it, Nora is flooded with memories of her twin sister— laughter mingling with arguments over who would keep the last remaining bear. For a fleeting moment, nostalgia wraps around her, igniting a bittersweet warmth.

After landing, exhaustion weighs heavily on her as she checks into her hotel, her heart still warmed by the hope of soon meeting her niece. But just as she begins to drift off, the hotel reception interrupts with devastating news: her twin sister has given birth, but the joyous moment turned tragic—her sister didn't survive.

Nora's heart crumbles, the weight of loss crashing down upon her like a tidal wave. In an instant, the holiday spirit is replaced by an unbearable sorrow, her dreams of celebrating new life intertwined with the sharp agony of grief. The laughter they shared, the plans for the future—all gone in a blink.

As Nora grapples with the haunting reality of being alone, the world outside continues to celebrate, unaware of her mourning heart. The silence of her hotel room becomes a sanctuary of despair, a distinct contrast to the joy she had envisioned. She is left with the profound emptiness of losing her other half, the one person who understood her completely. Christmas, once a symbol of hope and renewal, now stands as a haunting reminder of love lost and the bittersweet memories that will forever echo in her heart.

"Twin hearts beat as one, but in grief, one sister's tears can echo louder than joy."

-Hollie Dayes

In a nutshell: "The Tears of a Twin" is a poignant title that perfectly encapsulates the profound emotions in the story. It highlights the deep bond between the twin sisters and the heart-wrenching sorrow experienced by Nora as she navigates her grief during a time that should be filled with joy because of a new life. This sets the tone for a story filled with nostalgia, love, and heartache, exploring the complexities of grief and the enduring connection between siblings.

"Have you ever lost someone you love and wanted one more conversation, one more chance to make up for the time when you thought they would be her forever? If so, then you know you can go your whole life collecting days, and none will outweigh the one you wish you had back."

— Mitch Albom

Story 15:

When Santa Made Me Cry

It was the year 2017, Christmas Eve, six-year-old Jason sat by the window, his heart full of excitement, waiting for Santa, just as his dad had promised. His father, a police officer, had always made Christmas magical—dressing as Santa, bringing gifts, and making Jason feel like the luckiest boy in the world. But that afternoon, Jason's dad received a call from work; an officer had fallen ill, and he needed to fill in. Jason's parents had planned everything, so his father told him that Santa would be late this year because he had many gifts to carry.

Night fell, and Jason stayed awake, watching for any sign of Santa. Then, unexpectedly, his mother hurried him into the car. Jason could sense something was wrong, but his excitement for Santa dulled his worry. As they drove, the flashing lights of police cars and the wail of sirens filled the night. They pulled up near their house, and Jason spotted a police car parked on the side of the road. In the driver's seat, dressed in a Santa suit, was someone slumped over the steering wheel.

Jason's heart leaped with joy—Santa had come! He ran toward the car, his small legs pumping with excitement. But as they opened the door, Santa tumbled out, his face covered in blood.

Confused and frightened, Jason froze. He recognized the familiar figure through the blood-soaked costume—it was his dad. His hero. His Santa.

Tears welled in Jason's eyes as the world around him seemed to slow down. "Why isn't Santa giving me my gifts?" he wondered, his innocence battling with the horror of what he was witnessing. His mother rushed to him, pulling him close as he sobbed, his tiny voice trembling as he asked, "Mommy, why did Santa make me cry? Was I a bad boy?"

Later, Jason learned that his father had been chasing robbers and, in a final act of love, had stopped to change into his Santa costume to keep his promise. But the robbers had caught up to him and shot him, leaving him to die in the very suit meant to bring joy to his son.

That night, Jason lost more than his father—he lost the magic of Christmas, forever haunted by the memory of the day when Santa made him cry.

"A father's last promise once sparked joy, but reality shattered a child's innocence."

-Hollie Dayes

<u>In a nutshell</u>: This sad story emphasizes the tragic twist of a father's final attempt to fulfill a promise. The heartbreaking contrast between the joy and innocence of a child's expectations and the devastating reality that unfolded Jason's innocence.

CONCLUSION

As you turn the final page of *When Santa Made Me Cry*, the stories linger—haunting, yet filled with the quiet strength that only comes through enduring pain. These 15 stories have taken us beyond the surface of Christmas cheer, delving into the tender, hidden spaces where loss, heartbreak, and unexpected twists of fate dwell. But amid the tears and shattered hopes, there is something profoundly human in each tale— the quiet resilience, the fragile hope that continues to flicker even in the darkest moments.

Beneath the twinkling lights and festive cheer, these stories remind us that the holidays aren't always wrapped in happiness. Sometimes, they are marked by absence, by the weight of sorrow, by promises unkept and dreams deferred. Yet, amid the heartache, a deeper truth emerges: even when life brings us to our knees, we find ways to rise, to keep going. Every tear shed in these stories speaks of the resilience that binds us all, the fragile hope that is woven into them by sheer determination, an unspoken resolve to carry on despite the heavy burdens of life.

This collection doesn't offer easy answers or perfect endings. Instead, it reminds us that life, like Christmas, is complex and unpredictable, filled with beauty and heartache in equal measure. And in that complexity, we discover our greatest strength—not in the absence of pain, but in the courage to face it.

When Santa Made Me Cry is not just a book about loss, but about the quiet power of survival, the hidden strength that emerges when we least expect it, and the healing that follows even the most bittersweet moments of our lives.

REFERENCES

Keller, H (2019, November 26) Blissquote. *55 Famous quotes and sayings by Helen Keller*

https://www.blissquote.com/2019/11/helen-keller-quotes. html#:~:text=May%20these%20Helen%20Keller%20 quotes%20on

Lammott, A (2016, April 19) Womansday. Loss of Mother Quotes - Comforting Quotes About Death of a Mother

https://www.womansday.com/relationships/family-friends/ g39570031/loss-of-mother-quotes/

Montgomery, B. (1997, December 29) Soldier Quotes p.2 Azquotes.

https://www.azquotes.com/quotes/topics/soldier.html?p=2

<a href="https://www.azquotes.com/quote/203767" title="Bernard Law Montgomery quote"><img src="// www.azquotes.com/picture-quotes/quote-every-soldier- must-know-before-he-goes-into-battle-how-the-little-battle- he-is-to-fight-bernard-law-montgomery-20-37-67.jpg" alt=

Campbell, J (2018, September 5) Selfcarequotes.com line1 // military retirement quotes that will inspire you.//w.

https://selfcarequotes.com/military-retirement-quotes/#:~:text=Whether%20they%20say%20something%20about%20duty,

Cherry, B (2017, January 12) Your Tango. *comforting words of a mother who lost her child.*

https://www.yourtango.com/2020333840/comforting-words-mother-lost-child#:~:text=RELATED:%2050%20Beautiful%20Mother%E2%80%99s%20Day%20Quotes

Wadsworth, C. (2024, March 13) *Father and son quotes.* Good housekeeping website quote#56

https://www.goodhousekeeping.com/life/g27258933/father-and-son-quotes/

Knowes, L.R. (2012, February 10) Findyourmomtribe. 60 Encouraging Mom Quotes For All Strong Mothers Out There (findyourmomtribe.com) quote9

https://findyourmomtribe.com/encouraging-mom-quotes/

Kidman, N. (2021, April 3) 35 Words of Encouragement for Someone Going Through IVF - Happier Human.

https://www.happierhuman.com/words-encouragement-ivf-wa1/#:~:text=With%20all%20of%20this%20in%20mind,

James, L. (1995, July 27) Basketball player of the year.// Thedad.com 75 Heartwarming Quotes About Dads and Being a Father (thedad.com)

https://www.thedad.com/75-heartwarming-quotes-about-fatherhood/#:~:text=75.%20%E2%80%9CI%20want%20to%20experience%20being

Tolstoy, Leo (2012, June 27) Mothermindset. 15 Quotes About Losing A Child And Powerful Prayers For Healing (mothermindset.com). Psalm 30:5

https://mothermindset.com/losing-a-child-quotes/#:~:text=My%20prayer%20is%20that%20these%20are

Mofokeng, G. (2022, July 27) www.liveboldandbloom. 67 Fake Family Quotes To Help You Cope and Be Healthy (liveboldandbloom.com)

https://liveboldandbloom.com/03/quotes/fake-family-quotes#:~:text=Distancing%20yourself%20from%20fake%20family%20members

Davison, K (2022, March 17) Greatpetcare.com quote. Rescue Dog Quotes #1. Retrieved October 4, 2024, from

https://living.greatpetcare.com/inspiration/50-rescue-dog-quotes-to-celebrate-second-chances/

Johnson, M. (2023, May 24) Sad Relationship Quotes To Help You Cope With Your Feelings (thebridalbox.com) Updated June 20, 2024

https://www.thebridalbox.com/articles/sad-relationship-quotes/#:~:text=It%20is%20hard%20to%20get%20over

Ramone, M. (2021, December 20) Joincake.com/// missing-my-twin-quotes/ quote#5 Updated on April 23, 2024

Retrieved October 4, 2024, from the *Blogspot.*

https://www.joincake.com/blog/missing-my-twin-quotes/

Albom, M. (2023, March 21) Parade.com/ quote3.<u>55 Loss of Father Quotes to Offer Comfort - Parade</u> blogged by Kelsey Pelser

https://parade.com/1360617/kelseypelzer/loss-of-father-quotes/#:~:text=May%20you%20find%20comfort%20and%20peace

Drew, C. (2022, December 27) *Phrasedictionaryblogspot// metaphors for heartbreak*

<u>Metaphors for Heartbreak - (phrasedictionary.org)</u>

https://phrasedictionary.org/metaphors-for-heartbreak/#:~:text=%E2%80%9CA%20broken%20heart%E2%80%9D%20%E2%80%93%20This%20metaphor

www.ingramcontent.com/pod-product-compliance
Lightning Source LLC
Chambersburg PA
CBHW071024120626
46546CB00003B/1204